Original title:
Heartstring Happiness

Copyright © 2024 Creative Arts Management OÜ
All rights reserved.

Author: Adrian Caldwell
ISBN HARDBACK: 978-9916-90-648-4
ISBN PAPERBACK: 978-9916-90-649-1

The Chime of Happiness

With laughter in the air, we sing,
Moments bright, like birds on wing.
Sunshine dances on our face,
In joy's warm and sweet embrace.

Echoes of delight resound,
In every heart, pure love is found.
A melody that starts to rise,
Together, under endless skies.

Unseen Resplendence

In shadows lie the gems of hope,
Whispers soft, they help us cope.
Each hidden glow, a story told,
In silence, beauty starts to unfold.

A spark ignites the quiet night,
Guiding souls with gentle light.
Believe in what the heart can see,
For truth shines bright, eternally.

Free Spirits Together

Wild and free, we roam as one,
Chasing dreams under the sun.
With open hearts, we take our flight,
Creating magic, pure delight.

Bound by laughter, strong and true,
Exploring life in shades anew.
Every step, a dance we share,
In this journey, none compare.

The Glint of Kindness

A gentle touch, a warming smile,
Can brighten days and go a mile.
In small gestures, the world ignites,
Together, we spread the lights.

Each word of love, a seed we sow,
In hearts of many, kindness grows.
With every act, a shining thread,
We weave our care, where hope is bred.

Flickers of Joy

In the morning light so bright,
Small moments take their flight.
A child's laugh, a lover's kiss,
These little sparks, a simple bliss.

A warm sunbeam upon my face,
Nature's arms in soft embrace.
A shared glance across the room,
These tiny flames of joy resume.

Spirals of Contentment

Life's gentle turn, a quiet pace,
In stillness, we find our place.
Whispers of the heart's true call,
In every rise, there lies a fall.

Moments treasured, softly spun,
In the shadows, we've just begun.
A dance of thoughts, a steady flow,
In spirals, we find the glow.

The Symphony of Us

In harmony, our voices blend,
A melody that has no end.
With every heartbeat, rhythms play,
Together, we chase the gray.

In laughter's notes and whispers low,
The symphony continues to grow.
Each moment a chord, a sweet refrain,
In this music, love we gain.

Hues of Bliss

Colors splash in morning's light,
Painting skies with sheer delight.
Brushstrokes of laughter fill the air,
In every hue, love's bold flare.

From sunrise gold to twilight deep,
In vibrant tones, our hearts will leap.
The canvas of life, a bold embrace,
In hues of bliss, we find our place.

Whispers of Delight

In the garden where dreams dance,
Soft petals fall like chance.
With every breeze, a secret sigh,
Whispers of joy as hours fly.

Sunlight kisses morning dew,
Promises bloom in colors new.
Hearts awaken, hope ignites,
Moments cherished under heights.

Gentle hums of nature's grace,
Harmony finds its rightful place.
Nature's song, both sweet and light,
Whispers of delight in flight.

Through the twilight's soft embrace,
Magic lingers, leaves a trace.
Stars above begin to gleam,
In stillness, life becomes a dream.

Echoes of Laughter

Around the fire, stories spin,
Joyful faces, laughter wins.
Childhood tales, old and bright,
Echoes linger through the night.

Playful whispers greet the dawn,
Memories dance, never gone.
In the heart, a light remains,
Echoes of laughter in the veins.

Bubbles rise in cheerful glee,
Each moment shared, a jubilee.
Time may fade, yet we recall,
Echoes of laughter, the best of all.

Across the years, like a song,
Reminders of where we belong.
In our souls, the spark stays clear,
Echoes of laughter we hold dear.

Radiance in the Shadows

In the dimmest corners found,
Hope radiates without a sound.
Flickers of light dance and play,
Radiance brightens shades of gray.

Where fear hides in silent night,
Courage blooms, a guiding light.
Stars emerge to softly glow,
Radiance in the dark does flow.

Every heart bears scars so deep,
Yet in the dark, our dreams can leap.
Through the struggles, we will shine,
Radiance in shadows, pure and fine.

Let the dawn break through the gloom,
Life ignited, spirit soars to bloom.
With every challenge, strength will grow,
Radiance in the shadows, forever glow.

Serenade of Smiles

A melody of gentle grace,
In every heart, a special place.
With every note, the world ignites,
Serenade of smiles in the lights.

Laughter lingers in the air,
Moments captured, fond and rare.
With open arms, we share the bliss,
Serenade of smiles, a tender kiss.

Through trials faced and storms we brace,
A simple smile can find its space.
Bringing warmth where shadows creep,
Serenade of smiles, dreams to keep.

When darkness falls, let kindness reign,
A glowing heart can ease the pain.
Together, let our spirits rise,
In the serenade, our love never dies.

Tethered Joy

In the garden where the sun blooms,
Laughter dances in the air,
With every petal, joy resumes,
A tapestry of love laid bare.

Through gentle breezes, whispers play,
Hearts entwined, a sweet embrace,
In every moment, come what may,
We find our home, our sacred space.

Melodies of the Soul

In the hush of twilight's song,
Soft notes ripple through the night,
Each heartbeat a melody strong,
Guiding dreams toward the light.

Strings of fortune softly strum,
A harmony of hopes so bright,
In every silence, we become,
The echoes of pure, infinite flight.

Whispers of Delight

Amidst the stars, a secret sigh,
The universe sings our tune,
In every glimmer, spirits fly,
Dreams awaken 'neath the moon.

With every glance, a spark ignites,
Connection woven, warm and deep,
In blissful moments, pure delights,
We dance within the cosmos' sweep.

Strings of Contentment

In the quiet of a fading day,
The heartstrings hum a tender verse,
With every breath, we softly sway,
Finding peace in this universe.

Roots of kindness, deep and strong,
We gather 'round the evening fire,
In stories shared, we all belong,
Contentment blooms, our hearts conspire.

Dancing in Sunlight

Joyous laughter fills the air,
As we twirl without a care.
Golden rays upon our skin,
With each step, our hearts begin.

Nature's glow surrounds us bright,
Every moment feels so right.
In this dance, we feel alive,
In the sun, our spirits thrive.

Rays of Serendipity

Unexpected joy does bloom,
As laughter lightens every room.
Moments shared, so sweet and rare,
In the breeze, we feel the flair.

Connections spark in gentle ways,
Illuminating our days.
With each smile, the worlds align,
In serendipity, love shines.

Ties of Elation

Bound by joy, our hearts entwine,
In every moment, love will shine.
Hands held tight, we won't let go,
Through ups and downs, our bond will grow.

Waves of laughter, sweet embrace,
In this bond, we find our place.
Together facing all the trails,
Ties of elation never fail.

Canvas of Cheer

Colors splashed across the sky,
With each stroke, our spirits fly.
Painting dreams with every hue,
In this work, we find what's true.

Brushes dance with joyful glee,
Creating visions wild and free.
On this canvas, hearts will glow,
A masterpiece of love will grow.

Luminous Moments

In the twilight's gentle glow,
Whispers of the night bestow,
Stars awaken, softly gleam,
In this magic, we shall dream.

Fleeting hours wrapped in light,
Dance away the length of night,
Moments cherished, hearts entwined,
In this haven, peace we find.

Wings of Cheer

Brightly colored, laughter flies,
Beneath the vast and open skies,
Joyful echoes, spirits rise,
Kindred souls, no goodbyes.

Through the valleys, over hills,
Embracing life as the heart fulfills,
Every heartbeat, every sound,
In this cheer, our dreams abound.

Melody of Joy

Softly strumming, sweet and clear,
Notes that dance, bringing cheer,
Harmony in every sigh,
With each moment, hearts comply.

Songs of laughter, songs of light,
Filling days, chasing the night,
Together we create the tune,
Underneath the smiling moon.

Tapestry of Bliss

Threads of colors, woven tight,
In this fabric, pure delight,
Every stitch a tale to share,
Embroidered with love and care.

In the warmth of hearts' embrace,
Find the beauty, find the grace,
Life's rich hues in every glance,
In this tapestry, we dance.

Colors of Cheer

In gardens where the sun does play,
The yellow blooms make shadows sway.
With orange hues that light the scene,
And ladybugs, a joyful queen.

The sky above, a brilliant blue,
Holds whispers soft, the day feels new.
Violet dreams in twilight's gloam,
In every petal, there's a home.

Alive in the Moment

With every breath, the world awakes,
The laughter shared, a dance it makes.
Time stretches thin, yet feels so bold,
In stories shared, pure joy unfolds.

Between the beats, our hearts align,
In quiet whispers, love's design.
In fleeting thoughts that drift like air,
We find ourselves, beyond compare.

The Brightest Secret

Hidden deep where shadows blend,
A spark of light, the twilight sends.
Soft echoes sing of hopes embraced,
In silence held, the dreams we chased.

A shimmer just within our reach,
Life's mysteries, the heart can teach.
In every glance, a treasure holds,
A secret bright, the world unfolds.

Blossoms of Euphoria

In fields where wildflowers sway,
Each petal holds a bright bouquet.
With scents that dance upon the breeze,
Our hearts find joy among the trees.

Bright colors blend, a joyful sight,
In nature's hand, pure love takes flight.
Each moment shared, the spirit soars,
In blossoms sweet, the soul explores.

Laughter in the Breeze

Soft whispers dance through the trees,
Carried along with gentle ease.
Children's voices rise and flow,
Laughter mingles, soft and low.

Sunlight filters, casting glow,
A melody that breezes blow.
Joyful hearts in playful chase,
Finding magic in this space.

Clouds drift lazily in the sky,
As time slips past, we wonder why.
Moments treasured, sweetly teased,
In the laughter found in the breeze.

Radiance of Warmth

Golden rays kiss the morning dew,
A tender warmth that feels so true.
Embraced by light, the world awakes,
Each heart rejoices, no more fakes.

Shadows fade beneath the glow,
Hope ignites as feelings grow.
Every smile a spark to share,
Radiance blooms in the warm air.

Embers dance in the evening light,
Softly bidding farewell to night.
With gentle whispers, dreams unfurl,
In the radiance, our lives swirl.

Threads of Bliss

Woven softly, threads align,
Each moment holds a spark divine.
In gentle whispers, dreams take flight,
Binding hearts with pure delight.

Colors blend in harmony,
Stitching love through tapestry.
Every laugh, a vibrant thread,
In the fabric of dreams we've said.

Drifting through the vault of time,
In every stitch, the rhythm's rhyme.
A dance of joy, a swirling twist,
Forever wrapped in threads of bliss.

Echoes of Euphoria

In the distance, joy resounds,
Whispers echo, love abounds.
Over hills and through the trees,
Euphoria floats upon the breeze.

Each heartbeat sings a lively tune,
Underneath the shining moon.
Memories, like stars, do shine,
In the echoes, we intertwine.

Voices rise in sweet refrain,
Revelations born from joy and pain.
In the silence, we find our way,
Through echoes of euphoria, we sway.

Threads of Serenity

In the quiet dusk, peace weaves,
Soft whispers under the trees,
Gentle shadows brush the ground,
A melody that knows no bounds.

Stars awaken in the night,
Guiding dreams with silver light,
Every sigh, a sweet release,
In this moment, find your peace.

Through the stillness, hearts align,
In the tapestry of time,
Stitched with hopes and quiet grace,
We find our still, sacred space.

Through each thread, our stories flow,
Intertwined, we learn and grow,
In the fabric of the night,
We discover our own light.

Bouncing Bliss

A sunny day with skies so blue,
Laughter dances in the dew,
Children play, their spirits free,
Joyful hearts in harmony.

Bouncing balls and giggles loud,
Chasing dreams, they're feeling proud,
Each small leap, a big delight,
Turning moments into bright.

On the swings, they soar so high,
Touching whispers of the sky,
In their world, all worries cease,
Every moment brings them peace.

With every bounce, they find their way,
In the golden light of day,
Bouncing minds, unchained and free,
Purest bliss, simplicity.

The Playful Echo

Through the valleys, voices ring,
Nature's songs, a sweet offering,
Every call invites a dance,
In this game of wild romance.

Echoes bounce off mountain walls,
Joyful laughter, nature calls,
Whispers carried on the breeze,
In the rhythm, hearts find ease.

A playful spirit in the night,
Stars above shine ever bright,
Each reply a soothing balm,
In the dusk, the world feels calm.

Echoes of love, soft and clear,
Remind us that we're always near,
In this dance of joy, we sway,
Together, forever our play.

Golden Moments Stitched

In the tapestry of today,
Golden threads in warm array,
Moments captured, time enshrined,
Every heartbeat, intertwined.

Laughter shared around the table,
Stories woven, strong and stable,
Every whisper holds a spark,
In the light, we leave our mark.

Memories stitched with tender hands,
In this life, love understands,
Golden moments, bright and bold,
A treasure chest of joy to hold.

As the day drifts into night,
Soft horizons, warm and bright,
Each stitch binds what we adore,
In our hearts, forevermore.

A Defiant Grin

In shadows deep, a spark ignites,
With courage firm, it boldly fights.
A smile that breaks the stinging night,
A heart that dances, pure delight.

Against the storm, it stands erect,
With grit so fierce, it will protect.
A whispered hope beneath the din,
With every challenge, a defiant grin.

Harmony in Chaos

In swirling winds, the music plays,
A dance of life, in wild arrays.
Amid the noise, there's beauty found,
In disarray, a joyful sound.

Each note collides, yet we embrace,
This wondrous blend, a sacred space.
In chaos thrives a world so grand,
Where harmony walks hand in hand.

Glimmers of Joy

In morning light, the dew appears,
A soft embrace that calms our fears.
Each fleeting spark, a treasure's song,
In simple moments, we belong.

With laughter shared, and kindness spread,
In whispered dreams, where love is bred.
A gentle touch, a heartfelt sigh,
Together, we let joy amplify.

Prisms of Ecstasy

Through every prism, colors blend,
A kaleidoscope that will not end.
In vibrant hues, our spirits soar,
With every glance, we yearn for more.

Like rays of sun through autumn leaves,
In dazzling light, our heart believes.
This dance of joy, a wild spree,
In prisms bright, we are set free.

Flickers of Hope

In the dawn's warm light, we rise,
Whispers of dreams fill the skies.
Each heartbeat sings, a quiet prayer,
In the depths of darkness, we dare.

Through shadows cast, we find our way,
Painting the night with hope's soft sway.
With every step, the path unfolds,
The heart, a lantern, bold and gold.

Stars twinkle bright in the vast expanse,
Guiding us forward, a hopeful dance.
In the trials, we learn to cope,
Fueling the flames of flickering hope.

With unity strong, we stand as one,
Together we'll shine, like the morning sun.
Through storms and trials, we'll uplift,
With flickers of hope, the greatest gift.

Braided Laughter

In the garden where kinship grows,
Laughter weaves like a gentle rose.
Tales entwined with joy and cheer,
A playful echo we hold dear.

Round the fire, stories shared,
With every chuckle, no one spared.
Memories bloom like vibrant flowers,
Braided laughter, our finest hours.

In moments fleeting, we find our way,
A melody bright, come what may.
Through silly dances and warm embraces,
Our laughter flows to blessed places.

Together we rise, amid the strife,
Braided laughter, the thread of life.
With every giggle, our spirits soar,
In this tapestry, we are evermore.

Bubbles of Delight

In the breeze, bright bubbles float,
Each one dressed in a dreamer's coat.
They dance on air, shimmer and shine,
Capturing echoes of laughter divine.

With every pop, a wish takes flight,
Colors burst into pure delight.
Childlike wonder fills the sky,
As we gaze at the bubbles, nearby.

A moment captured, fleeting and sweet,
Tiny spheres of joy, a simple treat.
In the sun's warm embrace, we sway,
Bubbles of delight lead the way.

In the chaos of life, a gentle sigh,
We find our peace, as the bubbles fly.
Pure jubilation, so easy to find,
In bubbles of delight, joy intertwined.

A Journey to Euphoria

Step by step, we chase the light,
Through valleys deep, and mountains bright.
With hearts like compass, we roam free,
In search of what we long to see.

Whispers of wind guide our quest,
In nature's embrace, we feel blessed.
With every turn, a new view found,
A journey to euphoria, tightly bound.

The laughter echoes, a sweet refrain,
Through fields of gold, we dance in rain.
With hands held tight, we face the dawn,
In this journey, our spirits drawn.

As sunsets fade into twilight's glow,
We find our way where wildflowers grow.
In euphoria's grasp, we come alive,
With hearts wide open, we thrive.

Enchanted Moments

In the glade where shadows play,
Whispers dance in soft array.
Sunlight beams through leafy vines,
Time stands still as magic aligns.

Fluttering leaves in the breeze,
Nature sings with gentle ease.
Capturing dreams in twilight's hue,
Every heartbeat feels so new.

Stars awaken in the night,
Filling hearts with pure delight.
Every glance, a fleeting kiss,
In these moments, time's true bliss.

With your hand tucked snug in mine,
In this realm, our souls entwine.
Cherished memories softly glow,
In enchanted space, love will flow.

The Sweetest Symphony

Notes of laughter fill the air,
Dancing freely without care.
Harmonies of joy arise,
Underneath the painted skies.

Every heartbeat plays a tune,
Swaying softly like a balloon.
Whispers of love in the night,
Make our spirits shine so bright.

Melodies of longing shared,
In the silence, souls are bared.
Time drifts gently on the stage,
As we write our own new page.

Together, we create the song,
In this symphony, we belong.
Sweetest notes, forever sound,
In our hearts, true love is found.

Glistening Reflections

Morning dew on blades of grass,
Nature's jewels that come to pass.
Each droplet holds a secret bright,
Capturing the dawn's first light.

Rippling waters tell a tale,
Whispers carried by the gale.
In their depths, the world we see,
A calming, soft tranquility.

Mountains mirror skies so blue,
Painting pictures fresh and new.
In their shadows, dreams unfold,
Glistening like threads of gold.

Every glance a story weaves,
In reflections, the heart believes.
Nature's canvas, pure and free,
A tapestry for you and me.

Notes of Comfort

In the quiet of the night,
Soft and soothing, pure delight.
Gentle whispers, hearts inspire,
Wrapping us in warmth like fire.

A distant lullaby takes flight,
Embracing souls with tender light.
Each note brings a sweet embrace,
A sanctuary, a safe place.

Through the shadows, hope will rise,
Guiding us to morning skies.
In every phrase, the heart will mend,
Notes of comfort, love will send.

With every breath, we find our way,
In melodies of bright array.
Together, forever, we will stay,
In these notes, come what may.

Canvas of Light

In the dawn's soft hue, we find,
Brush strokes of colors entwined.
A tapestry of dreams revealed,
In every stroke, our fate is sealed.

Golden rays dance on the ground,
Whispers of beauty all around.
Each moment captured, vivid and bright,
Crafting a world with pure delight.

Clouds drift gently in the sky,
As laughter echoes, our spirits fly.
A canvas painted with love's delight,
Every heartbeat ignites the night.

With every glance, the heart takes flight,
In this wondrous canvas of light.
We gather moments, soft and sweet,
In the masterpiece of life, complete.

Embrace of Warmth

In a gentle hug, the world feels right,
Wrapped in comfort, banishing fright.
Sunbeams sprinkle on our skin,
A tender bliss, a sweet begin.

Fires crackle, stories unfold,
Nature's bounty, a warmth to hold.
Through the seasons, love will grow,
In every heartbeat, a steady glow.

Morning whispers, soft and slow,
A sigh of hope in the breeze's flow.
With every laugh, our spirits soar,
Embraced in warmth, forevermore.

In fleeting moments, time stands still,
Wrapped in kindness, the heart will fill.
Beneath the stars, our dreams ignite,
In the embrace of endless light.

Joy Unfolded

With laughter bright, the day begins,
Where every heart, a song, it spins.
In every smile, a tale to tell,
A gentle breeze, a soothing spell.

Children play in fields so wide,
Chasing dreams, with purest pride.
Laughter echoes in the air,
A melody of joy to share.

Moments sparkle, like stars at night,
Whispers of hope, our guiding light.
We dance through life, hand in hand,
With every step, in joy we stand.

From dawn to dusk, let spirits sway,
In joy unfolded, come what may.
Together we bloom, like flowers bold,
In the garden of stories yet untold.

A Garden of Gleeful Wishes

In a garden lush, where dreams will grow,
Gleeful wishes in soft winds blow.
Petals flutter, colors embrace,
In nature's cradle, we find our place.

Honeybees hum, a sweet refrain,
Their joyful dance erases pain.
Amidst the blooms, our hopes arise,
A tapestry spun beneath bright skies.

As sunlight bathes each leaf and flower,
We gather strength, in this precious hour.
With every heartbeat, love persists,
In this garden of gleeful wishes.

Let laughter blossom, let spirits soar,
In unity's glow, we will explore.
Together we'll weave our dreams anew,
In this garden, where wishes come true.

Light Beneath the Clouds

A glimmer shines in dusky gray,
Hope dances softly, lighting the way.
With every breath, the shadows part,
A gentle warmth ignites the heart.

Through veils of mist, a beacon gleams,
Whispering secrets, dreaming dreams.
In the stillness, peace unfolds,
A story of love, silently told.

Beneath the dark, compassion grows,
An ember stirs where kindness flows.
Rise up, embrace the soothing light,
For dawn shall break, dispelling night.

Echoing Laughter

In the meadows, children play,
Their laughter brightens up the day.
With every giggle, joy takes flight,
Chasing clouds, igniting the night.

Echoes bounce from hill to hill,
Each sound a song, a magic thrill.
In carefree moments, hearts unite,
Binding friendships in pure delight.

In every corner, smiles appear,
The world feels lighter, filled with cheer.
As laughter rings, let spirits soar,
For joy is meant to be shared more.

Sweet Resplendence

In gardens deep where blossoms bloom,
Colorful petals chase away gloom.
Soft fragrances whisper with grace,
Each vibrant hue, a warm embrace.

Dewdrops glisten in morning light,
Nature's palette, a pure delight.
Sweet resplendence, a sight to see,
Capturing hearts, wild and free.

As seasons shift and colors blend,
Life's gentle rhythm knows no end.
In every petal, stories flow,
A symphony of beauty to bestow.

Petals of Glee

Scattered dreams on the soft, green ground,
In every petal, joy can be found.
Colors burst like laughter at play,
Dancing softly, inviting the day.

A gentle breeze carries scents so sweet,
Nature's rhythm, a heartbeat's beat.
Petals twirl, like whispers of cheer,
In every moment, love draws near.

With each flutter, the spirit takes flight,
Embracing warmth in the morning light.
Petals of glee, scattered around,
In life's simple joys, peace can be found.

Wings of Laughter

In the air, joy takes flight,
Giggling hearts shine so bright,
Chasing dreams, we dance free,
Laughter echoes like a spree.

Together we weave our song,
In every note, we belong.
With each chuckle, spirits rise,
Wings of laughter, painted skies.

Moments shared, pure delight,
In the day, and through the night.
Kindred souls, we share a smile,
Wings of laughter, all the while.

Like a breeze that lifts us high,
Our dreams sail through the sky.
United, we light the spark,
In laughter's glow, we leave our mark.

Sweet Surrender

In the hush of twilight's embrace,
With tender hearts, we find our place.
Fingers locked, the world fades away,
In sweet surrender, here we stay.

The moon whispers soft and low,
Secrets that only lovers know.
In quiet moments, dreams entwine,
In sweet surrender, love divine.

Time stands still, a sacred pause,
In your eyes, I lose my cause.
With every heartbeat, tender grace,
In sweet surrender, we find our space.

As stars twinkle in velvet skies,
We dance together, love never lies.
Wrapped in warmth, our spirits soar,
In sweet surrender, forevermore.

Enriching the Ordinary

In a simple cup of tea,
Moments cherished, you and me.
Sunlight dances on the floor,
Enriching life forevermore.

A shared laugh, a gentle sigh,
Ordinary moments fly by.
Yet in their depth, we find the gold,
Enriching stories yet untold.

Walking paths both worn and new,
Finding beauty in the view.
In simple acts, our hearts engage,
Enriching life, a vibrant page.

Each day's rhythm, a sweet refrain,
Finding joy amidst the rain.
In every heartbeat, love's design,
Enriching life, your hand in mine.

Butterflies in the Mind

Whispers flutter, thoughts take flight,
Colors dance in soft twilight.
Ideas bloom like flowers rare,
Butterflies in the mind, they share.

In silence, creativity stirs,
Imagination softly purrs.
Chasing visions, oh how they twine,
Butterflies in the mind, divine.

Each whisper tells a story spun,
In the quiet, we come undone.
With every thought, a gentle wind,
Butterflies in the mind, they swim.

Let them soar on winds of dream,
Life's a canvas, paint the theme.
In vibrant hues and brilliant sign,
Butterflies in the mind, they shine.

Radiant Echoes

In whispers soft, the sunlight plays,
Through leaves that dance in golden rays.
Each beam a laugh, each shadow sings,
The heart takes flight on joyful wings.

Memories cling to warm embrace,
Like echoes in a sacred space.
With every spark, our spirits rise,
We chase the dawn, where hope lies.

Nature's song, a sweet refrain,
In every heart, it leaves a stain.
The world alive with vibrant hues,
In radiant echoes, we find our muse.

So let us roam, our spirits free,
In harmony, you and me.
With open hearts, we will explore,
The beauty that forever soars.

Windows to Joy

In every glance, a spark ignites,
A world of wonder in our sights.
Through panes of glass, we dare to dream,
Finding joy in every gleam.

Life's fleeting moments, framed in grace,
Each window opens, a different place.
With laughter shared, and stories spun,
A tapestry of hearts as one.

Colored light spills on the floor,
Inviting us to seek once more.
With every hue, a treasure found,
In windows to joy, we are unbound.

So take a breath, let love unfold,
In these frames, our hearts are bold.
With a gaze towards the vast unknown,
In each reflection, we are shown.

Candles in the Wind

Flickering flames, a quiet glow,
In darkest nights, they gently show.
A dance of light, through shadows we weave,
Candles in the wind, we shall believe.

Each tiny spark, a wish takes flight,
Chasing away the encroaching night.
With hope's embrace, our fears subside,
In fragile flames, our dreams abide.

When stormy gales threaten to drown,
We stand together, never down.
For in the flicker, we find our stand,
With candles in the wind, hand in hand.

So let us spark a new refrain,
With every flame, we rise again.
United bright, our spirits sing,
As candles in the wind take wing.

Gossamer Threads of Joy

In the morning light they gleam,
Soft as whispers, like a dream.
Each moment woven, bright and clear,
A tapestry of love sincere.

With laughter dancing on the breeze,
Joy's gentle touch puts hearts at ease.
In every glance, a spark ignites,
A world enchained in pure delight.

Through trials faced, we find the way,
In gossamer threads, we softly sway.
United souls in harmony,
We weave our song, a symphony.

So let the day unfold its grace,
In every smile, a warm embrace.
Together, in this vibrant glow,
We find our peace, our hearts in flow.

Serenade of Smiles

Beneath the stars, the night does hum,
A serenade, where joys become.
Each smile shared, a melody,
A song of love, eternally.

With every glance that lights the dark,
A laughter shared, a hopeful spark.
In quiet moments, hearts align,
In rhythm sweet, our souls entwine.

The moonlit path, our footsteps sing,
Joy's gentle touch, the warmth it brings.
In harmony, we find our way,
A serenade that brightens day.

So let the music never fade,
In smiles exchanged, a life portrayed.
Together, in this dance divine,
We celebrate, our hearts align.

Kaleidoscope of Happiness

Colors swirl in vibrant dreams,
A kaleidoscope, or so it seems.
Every turn reveals anew,
A spectrum bright, a joyful view.

With laughter bursting at the seams,
In every heart, a hope that gleams.
Together, painting skies so wide,
In every joy, we take our stride.

The beauty lies in each embrace,
In simple moments, finding grace.
With open hearts, let us explore,
A tapestry of joy, never bore.

In this dance of light and shade,
Happiness blooms in colors laid.
Together we will share the bliss,
In every hug, a perfect kiss.

Tapestry of Tranquility

In silence deep, the moments flow,
A tapestry where calm does grow.
With every breath, a gentle sigh,
In peace we find the reason why.

Where whispers of the wind do play,
And softest shadows dance and sway,
In nature's arms, we seek our rest,
A sanctuary, simply blessed.

Each heartbeat slows, the world retired,
In stillness found, our souls inspired.
Together here, we weave our dreams,
In tranquil times, life's sweetest themes.

So let the quiet fill our days,
In tranquil love, we'll find our ways.
Embraced in harmony's sweet balm,
A tapestry of life, serene and calm.

Emotions Set Free

In shadows deep, feelings stir,
Whispers of joy, a gentle purr.
Tears like rivers, flowing wide,
Hearts unburdened, dreams abide.

The weight of sorrow, lifted high,
Wings of solace, ready to fly.
Laughter dances on the breeze,
In every moment, we find peace.

In silence vast, thoughts collide,
Hope ignites, we no longer hide.
Embrace the chaos, let it flow,
Emotions bloom, a vibrant show.

Together we rise, unchained and bold,
Stories of courage, waiting to be told.
With every heartbeat, we claim our right,
To love, to feel, to shine so bright.

Raindrops of Felicity

Softly they fall, like gentle sighs,
Whispers of joy from cloudy skies.
Each drop a note, a sweet refrain,
Dance of happiness in the rain.

Children laugh with gleeful cheer,
Splashing puddles, with nothing to fear.
Nature's kiss upon the ground,
Raindrops of love, all around.

Colors burst in vibrant hues,
Life awakens, with every muse.
Each droplet tells a tale anew,
Of warmth, of joy, of skies so blue.

Embrace the storms, let them come,
In raindrops, we find a beating drum.
A symphony of life unfolds,
In the dance of raindrops, beauty holds.

A Heart's Mosaic

Fragments scattered, a beautiful mess,
Each piece tells a tale, no less.
Colors of laughter, shades of pain,
Together they form a vibrant chain.

Moments captured in a glance,
Memories weave in a wondrous dance.
Every loss, every love, a stroke,
Crafting the picture, as words invoke.

Through trials faced, we grow and learn,
In the flames of passion, bright hearts burn.
The mosaic shines, a masterpiece,
In the art of living, we find peace.

With every beat, the story flows,
A tapestry woven, as life bestows.
Embrace the chaos, the love, the strife,
A heart's mosaic, the beauty of life.

Shimmering Hopes

Stars ignite in the velvet sky,
Whispers of dreams, teaching us to fly.
Each shimmering light, a promise bright,
Guiding the lost through the darkest night.

In hearts aflame, aspirations rise,
Fueling the fire to reach new highs.
Holding our breath, we chase the dawn,
With shimmering hopes, we're never alone.

Beneath the surface, currents tread,
In the depths of struggle, hope is bred.
Through every shadow, we seek the glow,
In the search for meaning, we come to know.

So let the light guide your way,
Embrace the dawn of a brighter day.
With shimmering hopes, our spirits soar,
In the tapestry of life, we find more.

The Light Within

In shadows deep, our spirits glow,
A gentle spark, a warmth we know.
Through darkened halls, we seek the way,
The light within will lead the stay.

With every breath, it starts to rise,
A dance of dreams beneath the skies.
In moments still, it shines so bright,
Guiding us home through the night.

When hope feels lost, and paths are few,
Remember love, it's always true.
A flicker here, a flame anew,
The light within will see us through.

Together we can face the fears,
Illuminate the road with tears.
With hearts aflame, we'll rise and sing,
For in our souls, we hold the spring.

Woven Whimsy

In threads of laughter, dreams take flight,
A tapestry of pure delight.
Each color bright, a story shared,
In woven whimsy, love is bared.

The playful winds, they twist and turn,
With every heartbeat, passions burn.
A dance with time, so light and free,
In whims of joy, we find the key.

The whispers soft, of tales untold,
In every stitch, a world of gold.
With every weave, we find our place,
In woven whimsy, we embrace.

Through sunsets blush and morning dew,
Each moment's magic, we pursue.
In laughter shared, our hearts align,
Forever wrapped in love's design.

Kaleidoscope of Smiles

In every glance, a spark ignites,
A swirling dance of pure delights.
With laughter ringing, hearts unwind,
A kaleidoscope of smiles aligned.

The colors blend, a vibrant hue,
In joyful moments, born anew.
Each smile, a story, bright and clear,
In shared connections, we hold dear.

With simple acts, the world's aglow,
A chain reaction, watch it grow.
In kindness given, joy compiles,
Life's true beauty, a myriad of smiles.

Through every season, may we find,
The threads of love, so intertwined.
In unity, let spirits rise,
Together bright, our hearts surprise.

Tides of Contentment

Beneath the stars, where silence lies,
A gentle wave, the ocean sighs.
The moonlit path, a soft caress,
In tides of contentment, we find rest.

The ebb and flow, life's sweet refrain,
In every joy, in every pain.
With open hearts, we learn to trust,
In cycles deep, it's love that's just.

The sands of time, they shift and sway,
With every moment, come what may.
In tranquil waves, our spirits soar,
In tides of contentment, we'll explore.

As sun meets sea at dawn's embrace,
A sacred dance, a timeless grace.
With every breath, we find our song,
In tides of love, where we belong.

Unraveled Laughter

In shadows deep, where secrets lie,
A giggle bursts, it will not die.
Whispers echo, a playful breeze,
Together we dance, with twists and tease.

The world may mourn, in shades of gray,
But laughter blooms, come what may.
A thread of joy, so finely spun,
We weave a tale, of love and fun.

Like petals soft, a fragrant sigh,
Unraveled laughter fills the sky.
With every chuckle, bonds we mend,
In this embrace, there's no end.

So let us laugh, in twilight's glow,
In this sweet moment, our spirits flow.
With heartbeats quick, our souls ignite,
Unraveled laughter, pure delight.

Blooming Heartbeats

In gardens lush, where flowers grow,
Each heartbeat sings, a vibrant show.
Petals unfurl, in softest light,
Yet, shadows linger, just out of sight.

With every breath, new colors rise,
A symphony painted 'neath endless skies.
Nature's pulse, in rhythm divine,
We bloom together, your heart next to mine.

The fragrance sweet, the beauty rare,
In gentle whispers, we lay ourselves bare.
Rooted in love, we'll never part,
With blooming heartbeats, we start anew.

The seasons change, but we'll abide,
In autumn's gold, in summer's tide.
Together we thrive, in life's embrace,
Blooming heartbeats, our sacred space.

Joy's Gentle Caress

In quiet corners of the day,
Joy's gentle caress finds its way.
A soft embrace, a fleeting glance,
We live in moments, a sacred dance.

With every smile, a spark ignites,
To guide us through the darkest nights.
Hands intertwined, we chase the sun,
In joy's embrace, we become one.

The laughter swells, a sweet refrain,
In shared tomorrows, we feel no pain.
The world may spin, the storms may roar,
But joy's gentle caress opens doors.

So cherish the whispers, the smiles we share,
In every heartbeat, we find our prayer.
Together we journey, through thick and thin,
With joy's gentle caress, we always win.

Frosted Sunbeams

In winter's chill, where whispers freeze,
Frosted sunbeams dance through the trees.
A glimmer soft, on blankets white,
Nature's magic, a pure delight.

We wander paths, on glistening ground,
With every step, a joy profound.
Laughter crackles, in frosty air,
Together we wander, without a care.

As colors bloom in spring's embrace,
We'll chase the frost, that left its trace.
With every sunrise, new dreams we'll weave,
Frosted sunbeams, in love, we believe.

So hold my hand, we'll brave the cold,
In frosted sunbeams, our story unfolds.
With hearts aflame, we'll find our way,
In this bright world, we choose to stay.

Quicksilver Dreams

In the realm where shadows play,
Waves of silver drift and sway.
Whispers soft as morning mist,
Touching hearts that once were kissed.

Moonlight dances on the sea,
Chasing dreams that long to be.
Time, a river, flows so fast,
Hoping moments somehow last.

Stars alight with fleeting grace,
In the night, we find our space.
Through the twilight, visions gleam,
Living in our quicksilver dream.

Fleeting thoughts like fireflies,
Illuminate the midnight skies.
In this dance of life and time,
We find joy in every rhyme.

Brightening Grey

Clouds gather in a soft embrace,
Wrapping earth in a tender lace.
Yet amidst the shades of gloom,
Hope blossoms, a fragrant bloom.

Raindrops fall like whispered sighs,
Cleansing hearts, letting spirits rise.
From the grey, a vibrant hue,
Life returns, refreshed and new.

As the sun breaks through the night,
Casting shadows into light.
In this dance of dark and bright,
We find peace in every sight.

Brightening grey, our souls take flight,
Chasing dreams in morning light.
Nature's canvas, a vivid show,
Painting joy in every flow.

Rhapsody of Sweet Memories

Echoes linger in the air,
Softly woven, fine and rare.
Moments cherished, time won't steal,
In our hearts, they softly heal.

Laughter dances, sweet refrain,
Carried on the gentle train.
Every whisper, every glance,
Turns to music in a dance.

Through the halls of yesteryears,
Memories wrapped in joyful tears.
In the rhapsody we find,
Beauty fluttering, intertwined.

Holding on to what we love,
Guided by the stars above.
In each heartbeat, echoes beat,
Rhapsody of memories sweet.

The Joyful Canvas

Strokes of color, bright and bold,
Whispers of a tale retold.
On the canvas, dreams ignite,
Bringing forth the purest light.

Every hue a vibrant song,
In this world where we belong.
With each brush, we paint our fate,
Creating moments, small and great.

Laughter splashes, joy revealed,
In this work, our hearts are healed.
Dancing colors, wild and free,
Life's masterpiece, you and me.

The joyful canvas, wide and vast,
Holds our hopes, our dreams amassed.
In every stroke, our spirits rise,
Chasing sunsets, painted skies.

Dance of the Elated

In twilight's embrace, we twirl and spin,
Hearts beating wild, letting joy in.
With laughter as our guiding star,
We dance through the night, no worries, no scar.

The world fades away, just you and me,
As we sway to the rhythm, so free.
With every step, we ignite the air,
A dance of the elated, a love rare.

Our shadows blend in the silver light,
Winged whispers carry us into the night.
Together we leap, in perfect sync,
In the depth of the moment, we dare to think.

So let the music play, let spirits soar,
In this joyful dance, we crave for more.
As the stars above keep watch on high,
We step into dreams, just you and I.

Threads of Sunshine

Woven through mornings, golden and bright,
Threads of sunshine dance in soft light.
Each beam a promise, warm and true,
Painting the world in hues of blue.

Tangled in laughter, we find our way,
Chasing the moments of a sunlit day.
With colors bursting in a joyous array,
Threads of sunshine guide us, come what may.

Embraced by warmth, our spirits ignite,
We gather the memories, holding them tight.
With every heartbeat, we weave a new tale,
Threads of sunshine unfurling, we shall not pale.

As the sun dips low, the night softly sighs,
We carry the glow, where shadows arise.
In the tapestry of life, we'll always find,
Threads of sunshine, forever entwined.

Sparkling in the Gloom

In shadows deep, a flicker glows,
A light persists, where darkness flows.
With whispers soft, we dare to dream,
Sparkling in the gloom, a hidden theme.

Through tangled trails, we forge ahead,
Finding the spark when hope is shed.
Against the night, our spirits gleam,
In the depths of silence, we find our beam.

The stars might hide, but we will chase,
Each twinkle a promise, a sweet embrace.
With laughter echoing, fear takes flight,
Sparkling in the gloom, we ignite the night.

So hold my hand, let's face the unknown,
Together we'll shine, no longer alone.
In every shadow, a chance to bloom,
Forever we'll linger, sparkling in the gloom.

A Symphony of Grins

In a world so loud, we find our sound,
A symphony of grins that knows no bounds.
With laughter like music, we collide,
Creating moments, side by side.

Each smile a note in the grand array,
We play together, come what may.
In harmony bright, our spirits rise,
Through the joy-filled air, our laughter flies.

Like gentle waves on a sunlit shore,
A rhythm of happiness, forever more.
With every giggle, we light the scene,
In this beautiful dance, where dreams convene.

So let the melody carry us through,
A symphony of grins, just me and you.
With each cherished moment, we'll always know,
In the heart of our laughter, true love will grow.

Embrace of Light

In dawn's soft glow, we rise anew,
Warm rays dance bright, as dreams break through.
With every step, the shadows flee,
A radiant path, for you and me.

The sun spills gold on whispering leaves,
Nature's canvas, where magic weaves.
Together we bask, our spirits free,
In the embrace of light, eternally.

The morning dew, a promise made,
In gentle hues, our fears will fade.
Each warmth-filled moment, a treasure shared,
Two souls unite, a bond prepared.

As twilight falls, the stars align,
Their shimmering grace, a love divine.
In every heartbeat, the world ignites,
Bound forever in the embrace of light.

Harmonies of the Heart

In whispered dreams, our voices blend,
Soft notes ring out, no need to mend.
Each glance a song, a melody sweet,
In the dance of laughter, our spirits meet.

Through trials faced, we sing our truth,
The chords of love, the song of youth.
Together we rise, through joy and pain,
In harmonies of the heart, we remain.

The rhythm flows like a gentle stream,
In every heartbeat, a love supreme.
With every tear, a note of grace,
In perfect tune, our hearts embrace.

As dusk sets in, the chorus swells,
In starlit nights, our love compels.
Forever entwined in this sweet refrain,
In harmonies of the heart, we gain.

Joy's Gentle Embrace

Morning breaks with laughter bright,
A world of wonder, pure delight.
In every smile, a spark ignites,
Joy's gentle embrace, our hearts take flight.

Through fields of gold, we run and play,
Chasing dreams that light the way.
With every hug, each word we share,
A tapestry woven with love and care.

The sun dips low, its warmth still near,
In cozy moments, we hold so dear.
With laughter's echo, our worries cease,
In joy's gentle embrace, we find our peace.

As starlight twinkling paints the night,
In harmony, our souls unite.
With every breath, our spirits sway,
In joy's gentle embrace, forever stay.

Bubbles of Laughter

In a world of whimsy, we take flight,
With bubbles of laughter, our hearts ignite.
Each pop a giggle, each twirl a spree,
A symphony of joy, just you and me.

Through sunlit days, our spirits soar,
Chasing the echoes to the ocean's shore.
In frothy waves, we splash and scream,
Bubbles of laughter, a shared dream.

From silly games to secrets shared,
With every chuckle, a bond declared.
As time flows by, forever will we,
Dance with the joy in life's jubilee.

In twilight's glow, as shadows play,
Bubbles of laughter light the way.
Through every moment, a treasure amassed,
In this joyous realm, may we always last.

Milton Keynes UK
Ingram Content Group UK Ltd.
UKHW031319271124
451618UK00007B/228